My First NFL Book

BALTIMORE RAVENS

Steven M. Karras

LET'S READ
AV²
BY WEIGL™
ADDED VALUE • AUDIO VISUAL

Go to **www.av2books.com**, and enter this book's unique code.

BOOK CODE

Z742893

AV² by Weigl brings you media enhanced books that support active learning.

AV² provides enriched content that supplements and complements this book. Weigl's AV² books strive to create inspired learning and engage young minds in a total learning experience.

Your AV² Media Enhanced books come alive with...

Audio
Listen to sections of the book read aloud.

Video
Watch informative video clips.

Embedded Weblinks
Gain additional information for research.

Try This!
Complete activities and hands-on experiments.

Key Words
Study vocabulary, and complete a matching word activity.

Quizzes
Test your knowledge.

Slide Show
View images and captions, and prepare a presentation.

... and much, much more!

Published by AV² by Weigl
350 5th Avenue, 59th Floor
New York, NY 10118

Website: www.av2books.com

Library of Congress Control Number: 2017930535

ISBN 978-1-4896-5481-6 (hardcover)
ISBN 978-1-4896-5483-0 (multi-user eBook)

Printed in the United States of America in Brainerd, Minnesota
1 2 3 4 5 6 7 8 9 0 21 20 19 18 17

032017
020317

Editor: Katie Gillespie
Art Director: Terry Paulhus

Weigl acknowledges Getty Images and iStock as the primary image suppliers for this title.

My First NFL Book

BALTIMORE RAVENS

CONTENTS

Team History

The Baltimore Ravens joined the NFL in 1996. Baltimore had not had an NFL team for 12 years. The team is named after a poem called *The Raven* by Edgar Allan Poe. This is the only NFL team named after a poem.

Receiver Michael Jackson made 14 touchdown catches during the Ravens' first season. This was the most in the NFL that year.

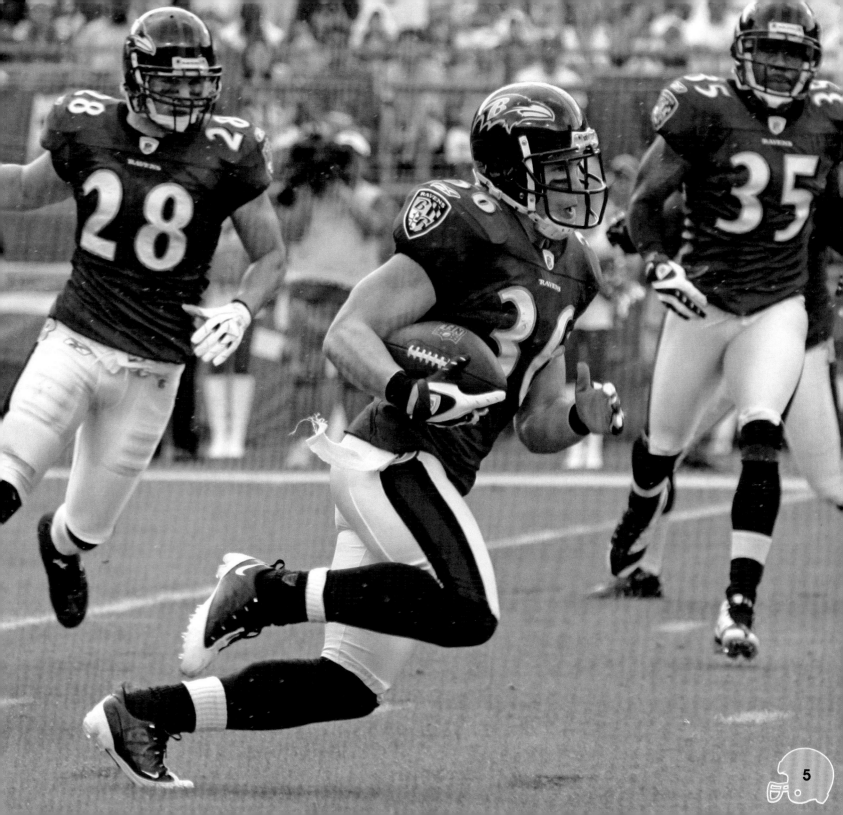

The Stadium

The Ravens have played at M&T Bank Stadium since 1997. The stadium can seat 71,008 people. There are five levels of seating. The stadium's two video screens are each 24 feet high and 100 feet wide.

M&T Bank Stadium in Baltimore, Maryland, is near the city's Major League Baseball stadium.

Team Spirit

The Ravens' mascot is Poe. He is named after the writer. Poe leads the team onto the field at the start of every game. He also brings the Ravens' team spirit to schools and hospitals in Baltimore.

The team has two real ravens who live at the Maryland Zoo.

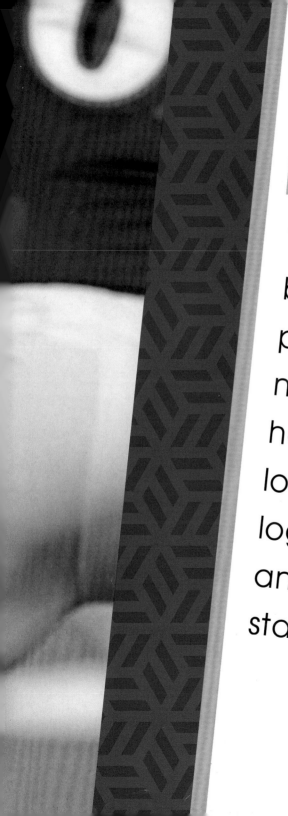

The Jerseys

The Ravens' colors are purple, black, and gold. Players wear purple jerseys with white numbers when they play at home. The team's second logo is on both sleeves. This logo has the same designs and colors as the Maryland state flag.

The Helmet

The Ravens' helmets are black with two purple stripes down the center. The team's main logo is on both sides of the helmet. This logo is a purple raven's head with a gold letter "B" in the middle of it. The "B" stands for "Baltimore."

A company called Riddell was the official maker of NFL helmets from 1989 to 2013.

The Coach

John Harbaugh became the Ravens' head coach in 2008. The team had an 11–5 winning record in his first season. Harbaugh was head coach when the Ravens beat the San Francisco 49ers in the 2013 Super Bowl. His brother Jim was the 49ers' head coach. The game was called the "Harbowl."

Player Positions

The center position is part of the offensive line. This player starts each play by giving the ball to the quarterback. The center also talks to the quarterback about what play to make.

More people in the United States watch the NFL Super Bowl than any other TV event.

Joe Flacco is the Ravens' quarterback. His first season was 2008. He was the quarterback during the team's 2013 Super Bowl win. He was named Most Valuable Player after that game. Flacco is the only quarterback in NFL history to win a playoff game in each of his first five seasons. His longest pass was 95 yards.

Jamal Lewis was a running back. He helped the team win the 2001 Super Bowl. He ran with the ball for more than 100 yards and scored a touchdown during that game. He also ran with the ball for 295 yards in a single game. This broke an NFL record. Lewis was named NFL Offensive Player of the Year in 2003.

Team Records

The Ravens have played in and won two Super Bowls. Fullback Le'Ron McClain set a team record in the 2008 season. He ran with the ball for 902 yards and scored 10 touchdowns. Receiver Jacoby Jones set an NFL record in the 2013 Super Bowl. He returned a kickoff for a 108-yard touchdown.

Jacoby Jones

108-Yard Kickoff Return

Le'Ron McClain

902 Yards and 10 Touchdowns

2 Super Bowl Wins

21

By the Numbers

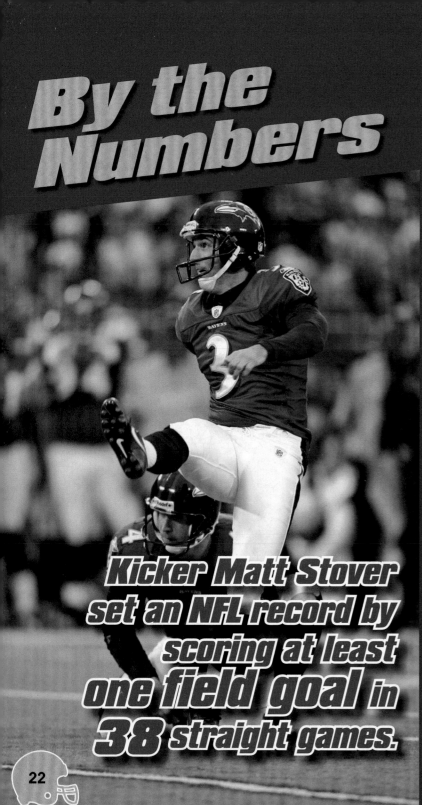

Kicker Matt Stover set an NFL record by scoring at least one field goal in 38 straight games.

Ray Lewis played his entire **17-year** career with the Ravens.

The most points the Ravens have scored in a single game is

55.

200,000 Ravens fans went to the 2013 Super Bowl parade in Baltimore.

Wide receiver Derrick Mason set a team record with **5,777** receiving yards in his career.

M&T Bank Stadium cost **$220 million** to build.

Quiz

1. Who wrote *The Raven*?

2. How many seating levels does M&T Bank Stadium have?

3. Where do the team's two real ravens live?

4. Who was named NFL Offensive Player of the Year in 2003?

5. How many fans went to the Super Bowl parade in 2013?

MEDIA ENHANCED BOOKS
AV² BY WEIGL™
ADDED VALUE • AUDIO VISUAL

Check out www.av2books.com for activities, videos, audio clips, and more!

1 Go to www.av2books.com.

2 Enter book code. | Z 7 4 2 8 9 3 |

3 Fuel your imagination online!

www.av2books.com

24